STANDOUT SOLOS
FOR RECITALS

By MELODY BOBER

ISBN 978-1-70517-638-2

EXCLUSIVELY DISTRIBUTED BY

WILLIS MUSIC

HAL•LEONARD®

Visit Hal Leonard Online at
www.halleonard.com

World headquarters, contact:
Hal Leonard
7777 West Bluemound Road
Milwaukee, WI 53213
Email: info@halleonard.com

In Europe, contact:
Hal Leonard Europe Limited
1 Red Place
London, W1K 6PL
Email: info@halleonardeurope.com

In Australia, contact:
Hal Leonard Australia Pty. Ltd.
4 Lentara Court
Cheltenham, Victoria, 3192 Australia
Email: info@halleonard.com.au

PREFACE

As a teacher, it is always exciting to choose new music for my students. Books that offer a variety of styles, technical challenges and opportunities for musical growth in expression and interpretation. Engaging pieces that students will enjoy from the lesson to the recital hall!

I am hoping you will find this collection, "Standout Solos," a joy to teach and a welcome addition to your intermediate students' repertoire.

Best wishes,

Melody Bober

CONTENTS

Beneath the Stars

Melody Bober

Celebration!

Melody Bober

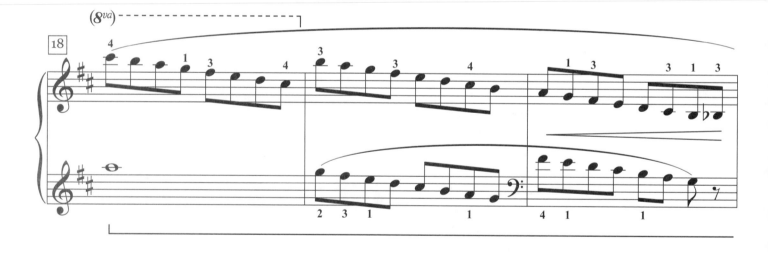

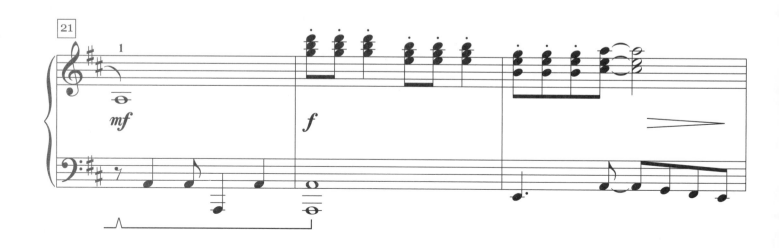

The Chase

Melody Bober

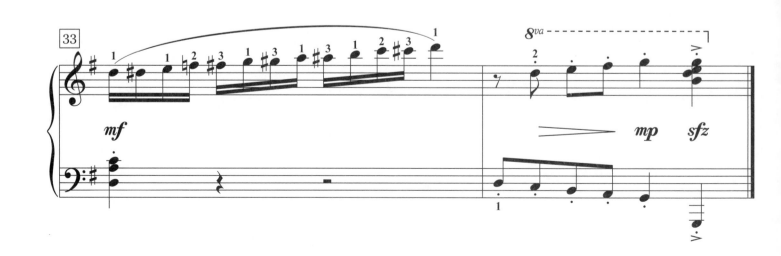

Fair Winds

Melody Bober

The Falcon's Flight

Melody Bober

Prelude in A Minor

Melody Bober

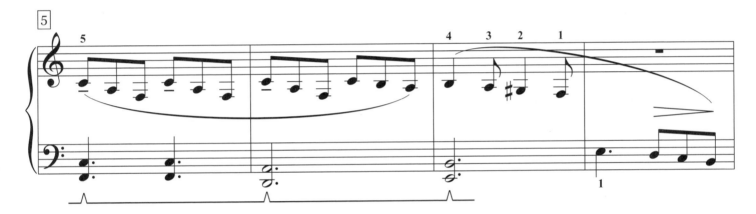

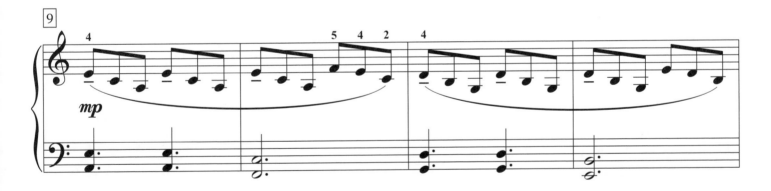

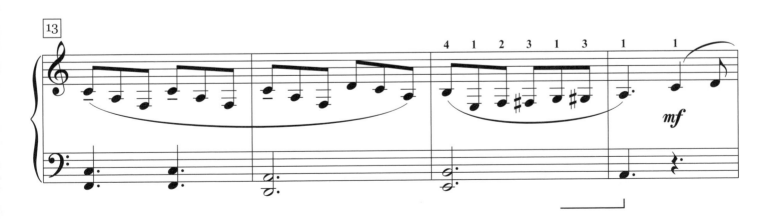

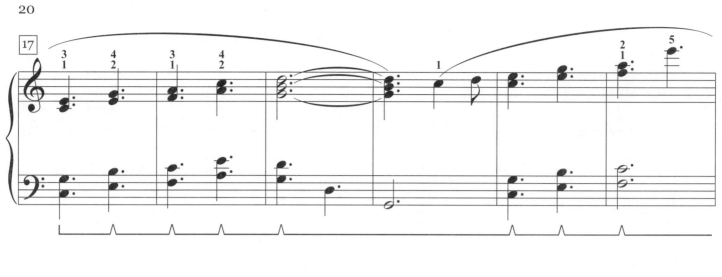

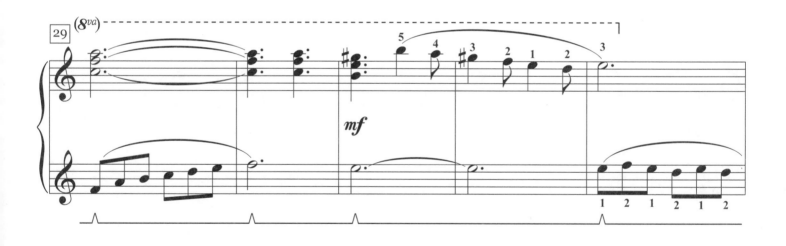

Fiesta Friday

Melody Bober

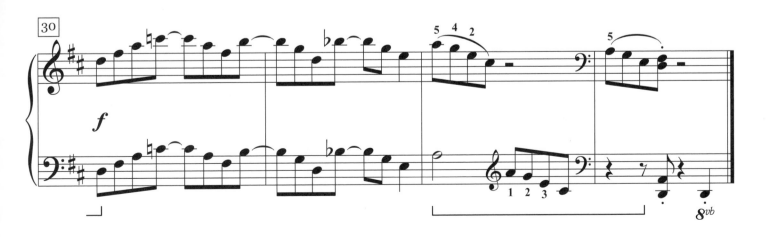

Moonlight Mystery

Melody Bober

A Sneaking Suspicion

Melody Bober

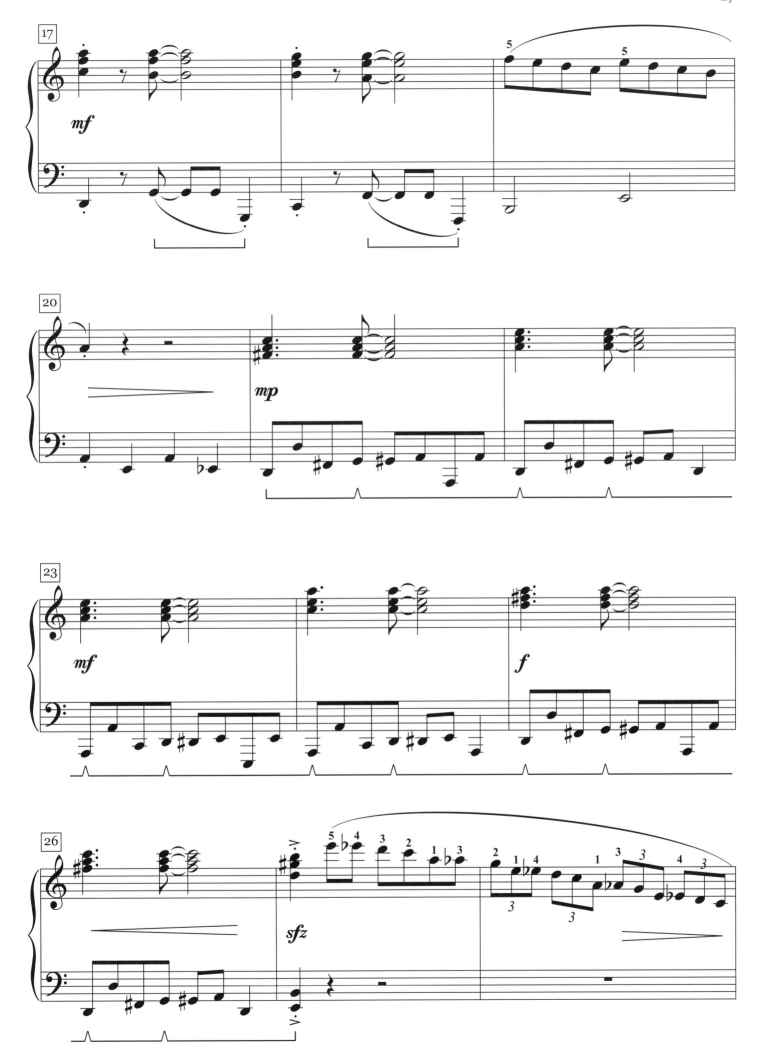

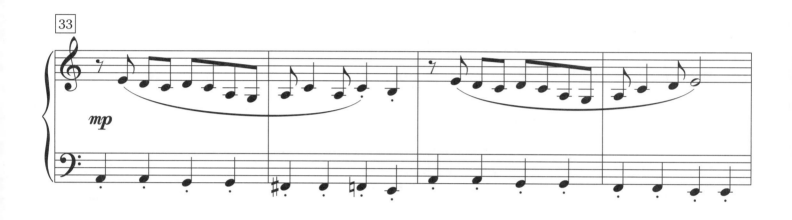

Snowy Wonderland

Melody Bober

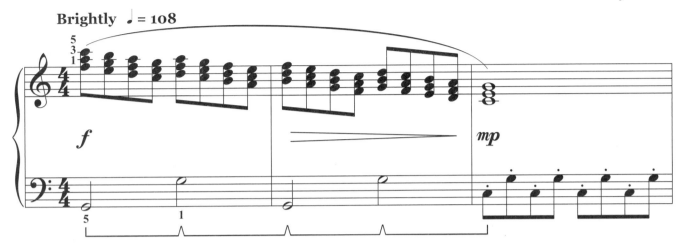

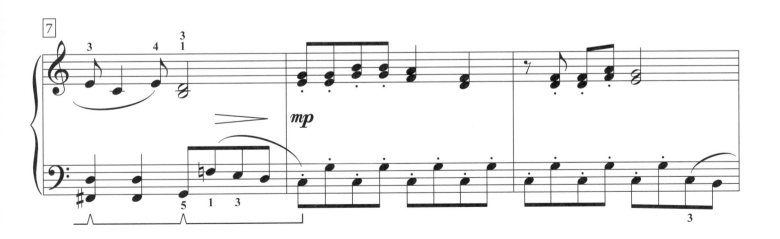

MORE EXCITING
PIANO SOLOS

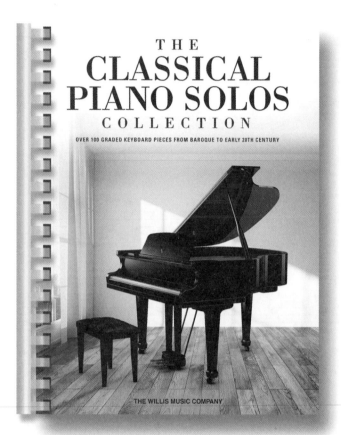

00289444 Classical Piano Collection

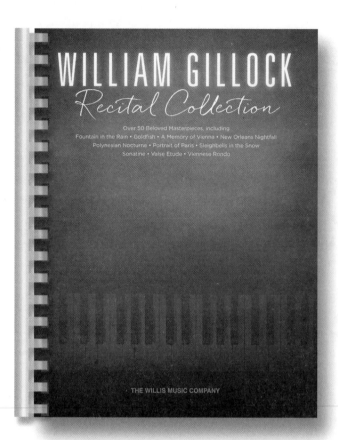

00201747 Gillock Recital Collection

00286619 Jazz Piano Basics Encore

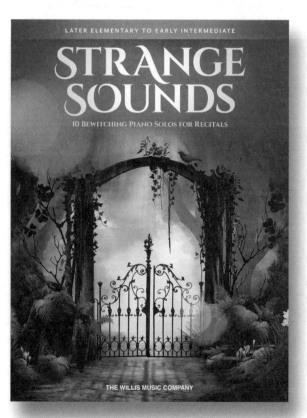

00373380 Strange Sounds